# WALT WHITMAN

Walt Whitman was born on 31 May 1819 on Long Island, New York. Without much formal education, he began work at an early age as an office boy, printer and school teacher. His first major collection of poetry, *Leaves of Grass*, was self-published in 1855. During the American Civil War, Whitman volunteered as a nurse at military hospitals in Washington, and his experiences inspired his next collection, *Drum-Taps*, published in 1865. This collection includes his elegies to Abraham Lincoln, 'O Captain! My Captain' and 'When Lilacs Last in the Dooryard Bloom'd'. His poetry was seen by many as immoral, and was the cause of his dismissal from a post as clerk in the Department of the Interior, but he won praise from his contemporaries Ralph Waldo Emerson and Henry David Thoreau, and his work was enthusiastically received by poetic circles in England. Having survived a paralysing stroke in 1873, Whitman left Washington for Camden, New Jersey, where he continued to write up until his death on 26 March 1892.

ALSO BY WALT WHITMAN

*Leaves of Grass*
*Drum-Taps*

WALT WHITMAN

# Song of Myself

VINTAGE

5 7 9 10 8 6

Vintage
20 Vauxhall Bridge Road,
London SW1V 2SA

Vintage Classics is part of the Penguin Random House group of companies
whose addresses can be found at global.penguinrandomhouse.com.

Penguin
Random House
UK

This version of 'Song of Myself' appeared in the first edition
of *Leaves of Grass*, published in the United States in 1855

www.vintage-books.co.uk

A CIP catalogue record for this book is
available from the British Library

ISBN 9780099595540

Printed and bound in Great Britain by Clays Ltd, Elcograf S.p.A.

# Song of Myself

[1]
I celebrate myself,
And what I assume you shall assume,
For every atom belonging to me as good belongs
    to you.

I loafe and invite my soul,
I lean and loafe at my ease . . . . observing a spear of
    summer grass.

[2]
Houses and rooms are full of perfumes . . . . the shelves
    are crowded with perfumes,
I breathe the fragrance myself, and know it and like it,
The distillation would intoxicate me also, but I shall not
    let it.

The atmosphere is not a perfume . . . . it has no taste of
    the distillation . . . . it is odorless,
It is for my mouth forever . . . . I am in love with it,
I will go to the bank, by the wood and become
    undisguised and naked,
I am mad for it to be in contact with me.

The smoke of my own breath,
Echoes, ripples, and buzzed whispers . . . . loveroot,
    silkthread, crotch and vine,
My respiration and inspiration . . . . the beating of my
    heart . . . . the passing of blood and air through my
    lungs,
The sniff of green leaves and dry leaves, and of the shore
    and dark-colored sea-rocks, and of hay in the barn,
The sound of the belched words of my voice . . . .
    words loosed to the eddies of the wind,
A few light kisses . . . . a few embraces . . . . a reaching
    around of arms,
The play of shine and shade on the trees as the supple
    boughs wag,
The delight alone or in the rush of the streets, or along
    the fields and hillsides,
The feeling of health . . . . the full-noon trill . . . . the
    song of me rising from bed and meeting the sun.

Have you reckoned a thousand acres much? Have you
    reckoned the earth much?
Have you practiced so long to learn to read?
Have you felt so proud to get at the meaning of poems?

Stop this day and night with me and you shall possess the
    origin of all poems,
You shall possess the good of the earth and sun . . . .
    there are millions of suns left,
You shall no longer take things at second or third hand
    . . . . nor look through the eyes of the dead . . . .
    nor feed on the spectres in books,
You shall not look through my eyes either, nor take
    things from me,
You shall listen to all sides and filter them for yourself.

[3]

I have heard what the talkers were talking . . . . the talk
    of the beginning and the end,
But I do not talk of the beginning or the end.

There was never any more inception than there is now,
Nor any more youth or age than there is now;
And will never be any more perfection than there is
    now,
Nor any more heaven or hell than there is now.

Urge and urge and urge,
Always the procreant urge of the world.

Out of the dimness opposite equals advance . . . . Always
    substance and increase,
Always a knit of identity . . . . always distinction . . . .
    always a breed of life.

To elaborate is no avail . . . . Learned and unlearned feel
    that it is so.

Sure as the most certain sure . . . . plumb in the uprights,
    well entretied, braced in the beams,
Stout as a horse, affectionate, haughty, electrical,
I and this mystery here we stand.

Clear and sweet is my soul . . . . and clear and sweet is
    all that is not my soul.

Lack one lacks both . . . . and the unseen is proved by
    the seen,
Till that becomes unseen and receives proof in its
    turn.

Showing the best and dividing it from the worst, age
   vexes age,
Knowing the perfect fitness and equanimity of things,
   while they discuss I am silent, and go bathe and
   admire myself.

Welcome is every organ and attribute of me, and of any
   man hearty and clean,
Not an inch nor a particle of an inch is vile, and none
   shall be less familiar than the rest.

I am satisfied . . . . I see, dance, laugh, sing;
As God comes a loving bedfellow and sleeps at my side
   all night and close on the peep of the day,
And leaves for me baskets covered with white towels
   bulging the house with their plenty,
Shall I postpone my acceptation and realization and
   scream at my eyes,
That they turn from gazing after and down the road,
And forthwith cipher and show me to a cent,
Exactly the contents of one and exactly the contents of
   two, and which is ahead?

[4]
Trippers and askers surround me,
People I meet . . . . the effect upon me of my early life
   . . . . of the ward and city I live in . . . . of the nation,
The latest news . . . . discoveries, inventions, societies
   . . . . authors old and new,
My dinner, dress, associates, looks, business, compliments,
   dues,
The real or fancied indifference of some man or woman
   I love,

4

The sickness of one of my folks . . . . or of myself. . . .
or ill-doing . . . . or loss or lack of money . . . . or
depressions or exaltations,
They come to me days and nights and go from me again,
But they are not the Me myself.

Apart from the pulling and hauling stands what I am,
Stands amused, complacent, compassionating, idle,
unitary,
Looks down, is erect, bends an arm on an impalpable
certain rest,
Looks with its sidecurved head curious what will come next,
Both in and out of the game, and watching and
wondering at it.

Backward I see in my own days where I sweated through
fog with linguists and contenders,
I have no mockings or arguments . . . . I witness and
wait.

[5]
I believe in you my soul . . . . the other I am must not
abase itself to you,
And you must not be abased to the other.

Loafe with me on the grass . . . . loose the stop from
your throat,
Not words, not music or rhyme I want . . . . not custom
or lecture, not even the best,
Only the lull I like, the hum of your valved voice.

I mind how we lay in June, such a transparent summer
morning;

You settled your head athwart my hips and gently turned
over upon me,
And parted the shirt from my bosom-bone, and plunged
your tongue to my barestript heart,
And reached till you felt my beard, and reached till you
held my feet.

Swiftly arose and spread around me the peace and joy
and knowledge that pass all the art and argument of
the earth;
And I know that the hand of God is the eldest brother
of my own,
And that all the men ever born are also my brothers
. . . . and the women my sisters and lovers,
And that a kelson of the creation is love;
And limitless are leaves stiff or drooping in the fields,
And brown ants in the little wells beneath them,
And mossy scabs of the wormfence, and heaped stones,
and elder and mullen and pokeweed.

[6]
A child said, What is the grass? fetching it to me with
full hands;
How could I answer the child? . . . . I do not know
what it is any more than he.

I guess it must be the flag of my disposition, out of
hopeful green stuff woven.

Or I guess it is the handkerchief of the Lord,
A scented gift and remembrancer designedly dropped,
Bearing the owner's name someway in the corners, that
we may see and remark, and say Whose?

Or I guess the grass is itself a child . . . . the produced
    babe of the vegetation.

Or I guess it is a uniform hieroglyphic,
And it means, Sprouting alike in broad zones and narrow
    zones,
Growing among black folks as among white,
Kanuck, Tuckahoe, Congressman, Cuff, I give them the
    same, I receive them the same.

And now it seems to me the beautiful uncut hair of graves.

Tenderly will I use you curling grass,
It may be you transpire from the breasts of young men,
It may be if I had known them I would have loved
    them;
It may be you are from old people and from women, and
    from offspring taken soon out of their mothers' laps,
And here you are the mothers' laps.

This grass is very dark to be from the white heads of old
    mothers,
Darker than the colorless beards of old men,
Dark to come from under the faint red roofs of mouths.

O I perceive after all so many uttering tongues!
And I perceive they do not come from the roofs of
    mouths for nothing.

I wish I could translate the hints about the dead young
    men and women,
And the hints about old men and mothers, and the
    offspring taken soon out of their laps.

7

What do you think has become of the young and old
    men?
And what do you think has become of the women and
    children?

They are alive and well somewhere;
The smallest sprout shows there is really no death,
And if ever there was it led forward life, and does not
    wait at the end to arrest it,
And ceased the moment life appeared.

All goes onward and outward . . . . and nothing
    collapses,
And to die is different from what any one supposed, and
    luckier.


[7]
Has any one supposed it lucky to be born?
I hasten to inform him or her it is just as lucky to die,
    and I know it.

I pass death with the dying, and birth with the
    new-washed babe and am not contained between my
    hat and boots,
And peruse manifold objects, no two alike, and every one
    good,
The earth good, and the stars good, and their adjuncts all
    good.

I am not an earth nor an adjunct of an earth,
I am the mate and companion of people, all just as
    immortal and fathomless as myself;
They do not know how immortal, but I know.

Every kind for itself and its own . . . . for me mine male
    and female,
For me all that have been boys and that love women,
For me the man that is proud and feels how it stings to
    be slighted,
For me the sweetheart and the old maid . . . . for me
    mothers and the mothers of mothers,
For me lips that have smiled, eyes that have shed tears,
For me children and the begetters of children.

Who need be afraid of the merge?
Undrape . . . . you are not guilty to me, nor stale nor
    discarded,
I see through the broadcloth and gingham whether
    or no,
An am around, tenacious, acquisitive, tireless . . . . and
    can never be shaken away.


[8]
The little one sleeps in its cradle,
I lift the gauze and look a long time, and silently brush
    away flies with my hand.

The youngster and the redfaced girl turn aside up the
    bushy hill,
I peeringly view them from the top.

The suicide sprawls on the bloody floor of the bedroom,
It is so . . . . I witnessed the corpse . . . . there the pistol
    had fallen.

The blab of the pave . . . . the tires of carts and sluff of
    bootsoles and talk of the promenaders,

9

The heavy omnibus, the driver with his interrogating thumb,
    the clank of the shod horses on the granite floor,
The carnival of sleighs, the clinking and shouted jokes
    and pelts of snowballs;
The hurrahs for popular favorites . . . . the fury of
    roused mobs,
The flap of the curtained litter—the sick man inside,
    borne to the hospital,
The meeting of enemies, the sudden oath, the blows and
    fall,
The excited crowd—the policeman with his star quickly
    working his passage to the centre of the crowd; .
The impassive stones that receive and return so many
    echoes,
The souls moving along . . . . are they invisible while the
    least atom of the stones is visible?
What groans of overfed or half-starved who fall on the
    flags sunstruck or in fits,
What exclamations of women taken suddenly, who hurry
    home and give birth to babes,
What living and buried speech is always vibrating here
    . . . . what howls restrained by decorum,
Arrests of criminals, slights, adulterous offers made,
    acceptances, rejections with convex lips,
I mind them or the resonance of them . . . . I come
    again and again.

[9]
The big doors of the country-barn stand open and ready,
The dried grass of the harvest-time loads the slow-drawn
    wagon,
The clear light plays on the brown gray and green
    intertinged,

The armfuls are packed to the sagging mow:
I am there . . . . I help . . . . I came stretched atop of
    the load,
I felt its soft jolts . . . . one leg reclined on the other,
I jump from the crossbeams, and seize the clover and
    timothy,
And roll head over heels, and tangle my hair full of wisps.

[10]
Alone far in the wilds and mountains I hunt,
Wandering amazed at my own lightness and glee,
In the late afternoon choosing a safe spot to pass the
    night,
Kindling a fire and broiling the freshkilled game,
Soundly falling asleep on the gathered leaves, my dog and
    gun by my side.

The Yankee clipper is under her three skysails . . . . she
    cuts the sparkle and scud,
My eyes settle the land . . . . I bend at her prow or
    shout joyously from the deck.

The boatmen and clamdiggers arose early and stopped for
    me,
I tucked my trowser-ends in my boots and went and had
    a good time,
You should have been with us that day round the
    chowder-kettle.

I saw the marriage of the trapper in the open air in the
    far-west . . . . the bride was a red girl,
Her father and his friends sat near by crosslegged and
    dumbly smoking . . . . they had moccasins to their

feet and large thick blankets hanging from their
shoulders;

On a bank lounged the trapper . . . . he was dressed
mostly in skins . . . . his luxuriant beard and curls
protected his neck,

One hand rested on his rifle . . . . the other hand held
firmly the wrist of the red girl,

She had long eyelashes . . . . her head was bare . . . . her
coarse straight locks descended upon her voluptuous
limbs and reached to her feet.


The runaway slave came to my house and stopped
outside,

I heard his motions crackling the twigs of the woodpile,

Through the swung half-door of the kitchen I saw him
limpsey and weak,

And went where he sat on a log, and led him in and
assured him,

And brought water and filled a tub for his sweated body
and bruised feet,

And gave him a room that entered from my own, and
gave him some coarse clean clothes,

And remember perfectly well his revolving eyes and his
awkwardness,

And remember putting plasters on the galls of his neck
and ankles;

He staid with me a week before he was recuperated and
passed north,

I had him sit next me at table . . . . my firelock leaned
in the corner.

[11]
Twenty-eight young men bathe by the shore,
Twenty-eight young men, and all so friendly,
Twenty-eight years of womanly life, and all so lonesome.

She owns a fine house by the rise of the bank,
She hides handsome and richly drest aft the blinds of the
    window.

Which of the young men does she like the best?
Ah the homeliest of them is beautiful to her.

Where are you off to, lady? for I see you,
You splash in the water there, yet stay stock still in your
    room.

Dancing and laughing along the beach came the twenty-
    ninth bather,
The rest did not see her, but she saw them and loved them.

The beards of the young men glistened with wet, it ran
    from their long hair,
Little streams passed all over their bodies.

An unseen hand also passed over their bodies,
It descended tremblingly from their temples and ribs.

The young men float on their backs, their white bellies
    swell to the sun . . . . they do not ask who seizes fast
    to them,
They do not know who puffs and declines with pendant
    and bending arch,
They do not think whom they souse with spray.

[12]
The butcher-boy puts off his killing-clothes, or sharpens
    his knife at the stall in the market,
I loiter enjoying his repartee and his shuffle and
    breakdown.

Blacksmiths with grimed and hairy chests environ the
    anvil,
Each has his main-sledge . . . . they are all out . . . . there
    is a great heat in the fire.

From the cinder-strewed threshold I follow their
    movements,
The lithe sheer of their waists plays even with their
    massive arms,
Overhand the hammers roll—overhand so slow—
    overhand so sure,
They do not hasten, each man hits in his place.

[13]
The negro holds firmly the reins of his four horses . . . .
    the block swags underneath on its tied-over
    chain,
The negro that drives the huge dray of the stoneyard
    . . . . steady and tall he stands poised on one leg on
    the stringpiece,
His blue shirt exposes his ample neck and breast and
    loosens over his hipband,
His glance is calm and commanding . . . . he tosses the
    slouch of his hat away from his forehead,
The sun falls on his crispy hair and moustache . . . . falls
    on the black of his polish'd and perfect limbs.

I behold the picturesque giant and love him . . . . and I
   do not stop there,
I go with the team also.

In me the caresser of life wherever moving . . . .
   backward as well as forward slueing,
To niches aside and junior bending.

Oxen that rattle the yoke or halt in the shade, what is
   that you express in your eyes?
It seems to me more than all the print I have read in my
   life.

My tread scares the wood-drake and wood-duck on my
   distant and daylong ramble,
They rise together, they slowly circle around.
. . . . I believe in those winged purposes,
And acknowledge the red yellow and white playing
   within me,
And consider the green and violet and the tufted crown
   intentional;
And do not call the tortoise unworthy because she is not
   something else,
And the mocking bird in the swamp never studied the
   gamut, yet trills pretty well to me,
And the look of the bay mare shames silliness out
   of me.

[14]
The wild gander leads his flock through the cool
   night,
Ya-honk! he says, and sounds it down to me like an
   invitation;

The pert may suppose it meaningless, but I listen closer,
I find its purpose and place up there toward the
    November sky.

The sharphoofed moose of the north, the cat on the
    housesill, the chickadee, the prairie-dog,
The litter of the grunting sow as they tug at her teats,
The brood of the turkeyhen, and she with her halfspread
    wings,
I see in them and myself the same old law.

The press of my foot to the earth springs a hundred
    affections,
They scorn the best I can do to relate them.

I am enamoured of growing outdoors,
Of men that live among cattle or taste of the ocean or woods,
Of the builders and steerers of ships, of the wielders of
    axes and mauls, of the drivers of horses,
I can eat and sleep with them week in and week out.

What is commonest and cheapest and nearest and easiest
    is Me,
Me going in for my chances, spending for vast returns,
Adorning myself to bestow myself on the first that will
    take me,
Not asking the sky to come down to my goodwill,
Scattering it freely forever.

[15]
The pure contralto sings in the organloft,
The carpenter dresses his plank . . . . the tongue of his
    foreplane whistles its wild ascending lisp,

The married and unmarried children ride home to their
    thanksgiving dinner,
The pilot seizes the king-pin, he heaves down with a
    strong arm,
The mate stands braced in the whaleboat, lance and
    harpoons are ready,
The duck-shooter walks by silent and cautious stretches,
The deacons are ordained with crossed hands at the
    altar,
The spinning-girl retreats and advances to the hum
    of the big wheel,
The farmer stops by the bars of a Sunday and looks at
    the oats and rye,
The lunatic is carried at last to the asylum a confirmed
    case,
He will never sleep any more as he did in the cot in his
    mother's bedroom;
The jour printer with gray head and gaunt jaws works at
    his case,
He turns his quid of tobacco, his eyes get blurred with
    the manuscript;
The malformed limbs are tied to the anatomist's table,
What is removed drops horribly in a pail;
The quadroon girl is sold at the stand . . . . the drunkard
    nods by the barroom stove,
The machinist rolls up his sleeves . . . . the policeman
    travels his beat . . . . the gatekeeper marks who pass,
The young fellow drives the express-wagon . . . . I love
    him though I do not know him;
The half-breed straps on his light boots to compete in
    the race,
The western turkey-shooting draws old and young . . . .
    some lean on their rifles, some sit on logs,

Out from the crowd steps the marksman and takes his
    position and levels his piece;
The groups of newly-come immigrants cover the wharf
    or levee,
The woollypates hoe in the sugarfield, the overseer views
    them from his saddle;
The bugle calls in the ballroom, the gentlemen run for
    their partners, the dancers bow to each other;
The youth lies awake in the cedar-roofed garret and
    harks to the musical rain,
The Wolverine sets traps on the creek that helps fill the
    Huron,
The reformer ascends the platform, he spouts with his
    mouth and nose,
The company returns from its excursion, the darkey
    brings up the rear and bears the well-riddled
    target,
The squaw wrapt in her yellow-hemmed cloth is
    offering moccasins and beadbags for sale,
The connoisseur peers along the exhibition-gallery with
    halfshut eyes bent sideways,
The deckhands make fast the steamboat, the plank is
    thrown for the shoregoing passengers,
The young sister holds out the skein, the elder sister
    winds it off in a ball and stops now and then for the
    knots,
The one-year wife is recovering and happy, a week ago
    she bore her first child,
The cleanhaired Yankee girl works with her sewing-
    machine or in the factory or mill,
The nine months' gone is in the parturition chamber, her
    faintness and pains are advancing;
The pavingman leans on his twohanded rammer—the

reporters lead flies swiftly over the notebook—the
signpainter is lettering with red and gold,
The canal-boy trots on the towpath—the bookkeeper
counts at his desk—the shoemaker waxes his thread,
The conductor beats time for the band and all the
performers follow him,
The child is baptised—the convert is making the first
professions,
The regatta is spread on the bay . . . . how the white
sails sparkle!
The drover watches his drove, he sings out to them that
would stray,
The pedlar sweats with his pack on his back—the
purchaser higgles about the odd cent,
The camera and plate are prepared, the lady must sit for
her daguerreotype,
The bride unrumples her white dress, the minutehand of
the clock moves slowly,
The opium eater reclines with rigid head and just-
opened lips,
The prostitute draggles her shawl, her bonnet bobs on
her tipsy and pimpled neck,
The crowd laugh at her blackguard oaths, the men jeer
and wink to each other,
(Miserable! I do not laugh at your oaths nor jeer you,)
The President holds a cabinet council, he is surrounded
by the great secretaries,
On the piazza walk five friendly matrons with twined
arms;
The crew of the fish-smack pack repeated layers of
halibut in the hold,
The Missourian crosses the plains toting his wares and his
cattle,

The fare-collector goes through the train—he gives
     notice by the jingling of loose change,
The floormen are laying the floor—the tinners are
     tinning the roof—the masons are calling for
     mortar,
In single file each shouldering his hod pass onward the
     laborers;
Seasons pursuing each other the indescribable crowd is
     gathered . . . . it is the Fourth of July . . . . what
     salutes of cannon and small arms!
Seasons pursuing each other the plougher ploughs and
     the mower mows and the wintergrain falls in the
     ground;
Off on the lakes the pikefisher watches and waits by the
     hole in the frozen surface,
The stumps stand thick round the clearing, the squatter
     strikes deep with his axe,
The flatboatmen make fast toward dusk near the
     cottonwood or pekantrees,
The coon-seekers go now through the regions of the
     Red river, or through those drained by the Tennessee,
     or through those of the Arkansas,
The torches shine in the dark that hangs on the
     Chattahoochee or Altamahaw;
Patriarchs sit at supper with sons and grandsons and great
     grandsons around them,
In walls of adobie, in canvas tents, rest hunters and
     trappers after their day's sport.
The city sleeps and the country sleeps,
The living sleep for their time . . . . the dead sleep for
     their time,
The old husband sleeps by his wife and the young
     husband sleeps by his wife;

And these one and all tend inward to me, and I tend
 outward to them,
And such as it is to be of these more or less I am.

[16]
I am of old and young, of the foolish as much as the
 wise,
Regardless of others, ever regardful of others,
Maternal as well as paternal, a child as well as a man,
Stuffed with the stuff that is coarse, and stuffed with the
 stuff that is fine,
One of the great nations, the nation of many nations—
 the smallest the same and the largest the same,
A southerner soon as a northerner, a planter nonchalant
 and hospitable,
A Yankee bound my own way . . . . ready for trade . . . .
 my joints the limberest joints on earth and the
 sternest joints on earth,
A Kentuckian walking the vale of the Elkhorn in my
 deerskin leggings,
A boatman over the lakes or bays or along coasts . . . . a
 Hoosier, a Badger, a Buckeye,
A Louisianian or Georgian, a poke-easy from sandhills
 and pines,
At home on Canadian snowshoes or up in the bush, or
 with fishermen off Newfoundland,
At home in the fleet of iceboats, sailing with the rest and
 tacking,
At home on the hills of Vermont or in the woods of
 Maine or the Texan ranch,
Comrade of Californians . . . . comrade of free
 northwesterners, loving their big proportions,
Comrade of raftsmen and coalmen . . . . comrade

of all who shake hands and welcome to drink and
    meat;
A learner with the simplest, a teacher of the
    thoughtfulest,
A novice beginning experient of myriads of seasons,
Of every hue and trade and rank, of every caste and
    religion,
Not merely of the New World but of Africa Europe or
    Asia . . . . a wandering savage,
A farmer, mechanic, or artist . . . . a gentleman, sailor,
    lover or quaker,
A prisoner, fancy-man, rowdy, lawyer, physician or
    priest.

I resist anything better than my own diversity,
And breathe the air and leave plenty after me,
And am not stuck up, and am in my place.

The moth and the fisheggs are in their place,
The suns I see and the suns I cannot see are in their
    place,
The palpable is in its place and the impalpable is in its
    place.

[17]
These are the thoughts of all men in all ages and lands,
    they are not original with me,
If they are not yours as much as mine they are nothing
    or next to nothing,
If they do not enclose everything they are next to
    nothing,
If they are not the riddle and the untying of the riddle
    they are nothing,

If they are not just as close as they are distant they are
    nothing.

This is the grass that grows wherever the land is and the
    water is,
This is the common air that bathes the globe.

This is the breath of laws and songs and behaviour,
This is the tasteless water of souls . . . . this is the true
    sustenance,
It is for the illiterate . . . . it is for the judges of the
    supreme court . . . . it is for the federal capitol and
    the state capitols,
It is for the admirable communes of literary men and
    composers and singers and lecturers and engineers and
    savans,
It is for the endless races of working people and farmers
    and seamen.

[18]
This is the trill of a thousand clear cornets and scream of
    the octave flute and strike of triangles.

I play not a march for victors only . . . . I play great
    marches for conquered and slain persons.

Have you heard that it was good to gain the day?
I also say it is good to fall . . . . battles are lost in the
    same spirit in which they are won.

I sound triumphal drums for the dead . . . . I fling
    through my embouchures the loudest and gayest
    music to them,

Vivas to those who have failed, and to those whose
    war-vessels sank in the sea, and those themselves who
    sank in the sea,
And to all generals that lost engagements, and all
    overcome heroes, and the numberless unknown heroes
    equal to the greatest heroes known.

[19]
This is the meal pleasantly set . . . . this is the meat and
    drink for natural hunger,
It is for the wicked just the same as the righteous . . . . I
    make appointments with all,
I will not have a single person slighted or left away,
The keptwoman and sponger and thief are hereby invited
    . . . . the heavy-lipped slave is invited . . . . the
    venerealee is invited,
There shall be no difference between them and the
    rest.

This is the press of a bashful hand . . . . this is the float
    and odor of hair,
This is the touch of my lips to yours . . . . this is the
    murmur of yearning,
This is the far-off depth and height reflecting my own
    face,
This is the thoughtful merge of myself and the outlet
    again.

Do you guess I have some intricate purpose?
Well I have . . . . for the April rain has, and the mica on
    the side of a rock has.

Do you take it I would astonish?

Does the daylight astonish? or the early redstart twittering
    through the woods?
Do I astonish more than they?

This hour I tell things in confidence,
I might not tell everybody but I will tell you.

[20]
Who goes there! hankering, gross, mystical, nude?
How is it I extract strength from the beef I eat?

What is a man anyhow? What am I? and what are you?
All I mark as my own you shall offset it with your own,
Else it were time lost listening to me.

I do not snivel that snivel the world over,
That months are vacuums and the ground but wallow
    and filth,
That life is a suck and a sell, and nothing remains at the
    end but threadbare crape and tears.

Whimpering and truckling fold with powders for
    invalids. . . . conformity goes to the fourth-removed,
I cock my hat as I please indoors or out.

Shall I pray? Shall I venerate and be ceremonious?
I have pried through the strata and analyzed to a hair,
And counselled with doctors and calculated close and
    found no sweeter fat than sticks to my own bones.

In all people I see myself, none more and not one a
    barleycorn less,
And the good or bad I say of myself I say of them.

And I know I am solid and sound,
To me the converging objects of the universe perpetually
    flow,
All are written to me, and I must get what the writing
    means.

And I know I am deathless,
I know this orbit of mine cannot be swept by a
    carpenter's compass,
I know I shall not pass like a child's carlacue cut with a
    burnt stick at night.

I know I am august,
I do not trouble my spirit to vindicate itself or be
    understood,
I see that the elementary laws never apologize,
I reckon I behave no prouder than the level I plant my
    house by after all.

I exist as I am, that is enough,
If no other in the world be aware I sit content,
And if each and all be aware I sit content.

One world is aware, and by far the largest to me, and
    that is myself,
And whether I come to my own today or in ten
    thousand or ten million years,
I can cheerfully take it now, or with equal cheerfulness I
    can wait.

My foothold is tenoned and mortised in granite,
I laugh at what you call dissolution,
And I know the amplitude of time.

[21]
I am the poet of the body,
And I am the poet of the soul.

The pleasures of heaven are with me, and the pains of
    hell are with me,
The first I graft and increase upon myself . . . . the latter
    I translate into a new tongue.

I am the poet of the woman the same as the man,
And I say it is as great to be a woman as to be a
    man,
And I say there is nothing greater than the mother of
    men.

I chant a new chant of dilation or pride,
We have had ducking and deprecating about enough,
I show that size is only development.

Have you outstript the rest? Are you the President?
It is a trifle . . . . they will more than arrive there every
    one, and still pass on.

I am he that walks with the tender and growing night;
I call to the earth and sea half-held by the night.

Press close barebosomed night! Press close magnetic
    nourishing night!
Night of south winds! Night of the large few stars!
Still nodding night! Mad naked summer night!

Smile O voluptuous coolbreathed earth!
Earth of the slumbering and liquid trees!

Earth of departed sunset! Earth of the mountains misty-
topt!
Earth of the vitreous pour of the full moon just tinged
with blue!
Earth of shine and dark mottling the tide of the river!
Earth of the limpid gray of clouds brighter and clearer
for my sake!
Far-swooping elbowed earth! Rich apple-blossomed
earth!
Smile, for your lover comes!

Prodigal! you have given me love! . . . . therefore I to
you give love!
O unspeakable passionate love!

Thruster holding me tight and that I hold tight!
We hurt each other as the bridegroom and the bride
hurt each other.

[22]
You sea! I resign myself to you also . . . . I guess what
you mean,
I behold from the beach your crooked inviting fingers,
I believe you refuse to go back without feeling of me;
We must have a turn together . . . . I undress . . . .
hurry me out of sight of the land,
Cushion me soft . . . . rock me in billowy drowse,
Dash me with amorous wet. . . . I can repay you.

Sea of stretched ground-swells!
Sea breathing broad and convulsive breaths!
Sea of the brine of life! Sea of unshovelled and always-
ready graves!

Howler and scooper of storms! Capricious and dainty sea!
I am integral with you . . . . I too am of one phase and
   of all phases.

Partaker of influx and efflux . . . . extoller of hate and
   conciliation,
Extoller of armies and those that sleep in each others'
   arms.

I am he attesting sympathy;
Shall I make my list of things in the house and skip the
   house that supports them?

I am the poet of commonsense and of the demonstrable
   and of immortality;
And am not the poet of goodness only . . . . I do not
   decline to be the poet of wickedness also.

Washes and razors for foofoos . . . . for me freckles and a
   bristling beard.

What blurt is it about virtue and about vice?
Evil propels me, and reform of evil propels me . . . . I
   stand indifferent,
My gait is no faultfinder's or rejecter's gait,
I moisten the roots of all that has grown.

Did you fear some scrofula out of the unflagging
   pregnancy?
Did you guess the celestial laws are yet to be worked
   over and rectified?

I step up to say that what we do is right and what we

affirm is right . . . . and some is only the ore of
    right,
Witnesses of us . . . . one side a balance and the
    antipodal side a balance,
Soft doctrine as steady help as stable doctrine,
Thoughts and deeds of the present our rouse and early
    start.

This minute that comes to me over the past decillions,
There is no better than it and now.

What behaved well in the past or behaves well today is
    not such a wonder,
The wonder is always and always how there can be a
    mean man or an infidel.

[23]
Endless unfolding of words of ages!
And mine a word of the modern . . . . a word en
    masse.

A word of the faith that never balks,
One time as good as another time . . . . here or
    henceforward it is all the same to me.

A word of reality . . . . materialism first and last imbuing.

Hurrah for positive science! Long live exact
    demonstration!
Fetch stonecrop and mix it with cedar and branches of
    lilac;
This is the lexicographer or chemist . . . . this made a
    grammar of the old cartouches,

These mariners put the ship through dangerous unknown
    seas,
This is the geologist, and this works with the scalpel, and
    this is a mathematician.

Gentlemen I receive you, and attach and clasp hands with
    you,
The facts are useful and real . . . . they are not my
    dwelling . . . . I enter by them to an area of my
    dwelling.

I am less the reminder of property or qualities, and more
    the reminder of life,
And go on the square for my own sake and for other's sake,
And make short account of neuters and geldings, and
    favor men and women fully equipped,
And beat the gong of revolt, and stop with fugitives and
    them that plot and conspire.

[24]
Walt Whitman, an American, one of the roughs, a kosmos,
Disorderly fleshy and sensual . . . . eating drinking and
    breeding,
No sentimentalist . . . . no stander above men and
    women or apart from them . . . . no more modest
    than immodest.

Unscrew the locks from the doors!
Unscrew the doors themselves from their jambs!

Whoever degrades another degrades me . . . . and
    whatever is done or said returns at last to me,
And whatever I do or say I also return.

Through me the afflatus surging and surging . . . .
    through me the current and index.

I speak the password primeval . . . . I give the sign of
    democracy;
By God! I will accept nothing which all cannot have
    their counterpart of on the same terms.

Through me many long dumb voices,
Voices of the interminable generations of slaves,
Voices of prostitutes and of deformed persons,
Voices of the diseased and despairing, and of thieves and
    dwarfs,
Voices of cycles of preparation and accretion,
And of the threads that connect the stars—and of wombs,
    and of the fatherstuff,
And of the rights of them the others are down upon,
Of the trivial and flat and foolish and despised,
Of fog in the air and beetles rolling balls of dung.

Through me forbidden voices,
Voices of sexes and lusts . . . . voices veiled, and I remove
    the veil,
Voices indecent by me clarified and transfigured.

I do not press my finger across my mouth,
I keep as delicate around the bowels as around the head
    and heart,
Copulation is no more rank to me than death is.

I believe in the flesh and the appetites,
Seeing hearing and feeling are miracles, and each part
    and tag of me is a miracle.

Divine am I inside and out, and I make holy whatever I
    touch or am touched from;
The scent of these arm-pits is aroma finer than prayer,
This head is more than churches or bibles or creeds.

If I worship any particular thing it shall be some of the
    spread of my body;
Translucent mould of me it shall be you,
Shaded ledges and rests, firm masculine coulter, it shall be
    you,
Whatever goes to the tilth of me it shall be you,
You my rich blood, your milky stream pale strippings of
    my life;
Breast that presses against other breasts it shall be you,
My brain it shall be your occult convolutions,
Root of washed sweet-flag, timorous pond-snipe, nest of
    guarded duplicate eggs, it shall be you,
Mixed tussled hay of head and beard and brawn it shall
    be you,
Trickling sap of maple, fibre of manly wheat, it shall be
    you;
Sun so generous it shall be you,
Vapors lighting and shading my face it shall be you,
You sweaty brooks and dews it shall be you,
Winds whose soft-tickling genitals rub against me it shall
    be you,
Broad muscular fields, branches of liveoak, loving lounger
    in my winding paths, it shall be you,
Hands I have taken, face I have kissed, mortal I have ever
    touched, it shall be you.

I dote on myself . . . . there is that lot of me, and all so
    luscious,

Each moment and whatever happens thrills me with
    joy.

I cannot tell how my ankles bend . . . . nor whence the
    cause of my faintest wish,
Nor the cause of the friendship I emit. . . . nor the cause
    of the friendship I take again.

To walk up my stoop is unaccountable . . . . I pause to
    consider if it really be,
That I eat and drink is spectacle enough for the great
    authors and schools,
A morning-glory at my window satisfies me more than
    the metaphysics of books.

To behold the daybreak!
The little light fades the immense and diaphanous
    shadows,
The air tastes good to my palate.

Hefts of the moving world at innocent gambols, silently
    rising, freshly exuding,
Scooting obliquely high and low.

Something I cannot see puts upward libidinous prongs,
Seas of bright juice suffuse heaven.

The earth by the sky staid with . . . . the daily close of
    their junction,
The heaved challenge from the east that moment over
    my head,
The mocking taunt, See then whether you shall be
    master!

[25]
Dazzling and tremendous how quick the sunrise would
    kill me,
If I could not now and always send sunrise out of me.

We also ascend dazzling and tremendous as the sun,
We found our own my soul in the calm and cool of the
    daybreak.

My voice goes after what my eyes cannot reach,
With the twirl of my tongue I encompass worlds and
    volumes of worlds.

Speech is the twin of my vision . . . . it is unequal to
    measure itself.
It provokes me forever,
It says sarcastically, Walt, you understand enough . . . .
    why don't you let it out then?

Come now I will not be tantalized . . . . you conceive
    too much of articulation.

Do you not know how the buds beneath are folded?
Waiting in gloom protected by frost,
The dirt receding before my prophetical screams,
I underlying causes to balance them at last,
My knowledge my live parts. . . . it keeping tally with
    the meaning of things,
Happiness . . . . which whoever hears me let him or her
    set out in search of this day.

My final merit I refuse you . . . . I refuse putting from
    me the best I am.

Encompass worlds but never try to encompass me,
I crowd your noisiest talk by looking toward you.

Writing and talk do not prove me,
I carry the plenum of proof and every thing else in my face,
With the hush of my lips I confound the topmost skeptic.

[26]
I think I will do nothing for a long time but listen,
And accrue what I hear into myself . . . . and let sounds
    contribute toward me.

I hear the bravuras of birds . . . . the bustle of growing
    wheat . . . . gossip of flames . . . . clack of sticks
    cooking my meals.

I hear the sound of the human voice . . . . a sound I
    love,
I hear all sounds as they are tuned to their uses . . . .
    sounds of the city and sounds out of the city . . . .
    sounds of the day and night;
Talkative young ones to those that like them . . . . the
    recitative of fish-pedlars and fruit-pedlars . . . . the
    loud laugh of workpeople at their meals,
The angry base of disjointed friendship . . . . the faint
    tones of the sick,
The judge with hands tight to the desk, his shaky lips
    pronouncing a death-sentence,
The heave'e'yo of stevedores unlading ships by the
    wharves . . . . the refrain of the anchor-lifters;
The ring of alarm-bells . . . . the cry of fire . . . . the
    whirr of swiftstreaking engines and hose-carts with
    premonitory tinkles and colored lights,

The steam-whistle . . . . the solid roll of the train of
    approaching cars;
The slow-march played at night at the head of the
    association,
They go to guard some corpse . . . . the flag-tops are
    draped with black muslin.

I hear the violincello or mans heart complaint,
And hear the keyed cornet or else the echo of sunset.

I hear the chorus . . . . it is a grand-opera . . . . this
    indeed is music!

A tenor large and fresh as the creation fills me,
The orbic flex of his mouth is pouring and filling me full.

I hear the trained soprano . . . . she convulses me like
    the climax of my love-grip;
The orchestra whirls me wider than Uranus flies,
It wrenches unnamable ardors from my breast,
It throbs me to gulps of the farthest down horror,
It sails me . . . . I dab with bare feet . . . . they are
    licked by the indolent waves,
I am exposed . . . . cut by bitter and poisoned hail,
Steeped amid honeyed morphine . . . . my windpipe
    squeezed in the fakes of death,
Let up again to feel the puzzle of puzzles,
And that we call Being.

[27]
To be in any form, what is that?
If nothing lay more developed the quahaug and its
    callous shell were enough.

Mine is no callous shell,
I have instant conductors all over me whether I pass or
    stop,
They seize every object and lead it harmlessly through me.

I merely stir, press, feel with my fingers, and am happy,
To touch my person to some one else's is about as much
    as I can stand.

[28]
Is this then a touch? . . . . quivering me to a new
    identity,
Flames and ether making a rush for my veins,
Treacherous tip of me reaching and crowding to help
    them,
My flesh and blood playing out lightning, to strike what
    is hardly different from myself,
On all sides prurient provokers stiffening my limbs,
Straining the udder of my heart for its withheld drip,
Behaving licentious toward me, taking no denial,
Depriving me of my best as for a purpose,
Unbuttoning my clothes and holding me by the bare
    waist,
Deluding my confusion with the calm of the sunlight
    and pasture fields,
Immodestly sliding the fellow-senses away,
They bribed to swap off with touch, and go and graze at
    the edges of me,
No consideration, no regard for my draining strength or
    my anger,
Fetching the rest of the herd around to enjoy them
    awhile,
Then all uniting to stand on a headland and worry me.

The sentries desert every other part of me,
They have left me helpless to a red marauder,
They all come to the headland to witness and assist
    against me.

I am given up by traitors;
I talk wildly . . . . I have lost my wits . . . . I and
    nobody else am the greatest traitor,
I went myself first to the headland . . . . my own hands
    carried me there.

You villain touch! what are you doing? . . . . my breath
    is tight in its throat;
Unclench your floodgates! you are too much for me.

[29]
Blind loving wrestling touch! Sheathed hooded
    sharptoothed touch!
Did it make you ache so leaving me?

Parting tracked by arriving . . . . perpetual payment of
    the perpetual loan,
Rich showering rain, and recompense richer afterward.

Sprouts take and accumulate . . . . stand by the curb
    prolific and vital,
Landscapes projected masculine full-sized and golden.

[30]
All truths wait in all things,
They neither hasten their own delivery nor resist it,
They do not need the obstetric forceps of the surgeon,
The insignificant is as big to me as any,

What is less or more than a touch?

Logic and sermons never convince,
The damp of the night drives deeper into my soul.

Only what proves itself to every man and woman is so,
Only what nobody denies is so.

A minute and a drop of me settle my brain;
I believe the soggy clods shall become lovers and lamps,
And a compend of compends is the meat of a man or
    woman,
And a summit and flower there is the feeling they have
    for each other,
And they are to branch boundlessly out of that lesson
    until it becomes omnific,
And until every one shall delight us, and we them.

[31]
I believe a leaf of grass is no less than the journey work
    of the stars,
And the pismire is equally perfect, and a grain of sand,
    and the egg of the wren,
And the tree-toad is a chef-d'oeuvre for the highest,
And the running blackberry would adorn the parlors of
    heaven,
And the narrowest hinge in my hand puts to scorn all
    machinery,
And the cow crunching with depressed head surpasses
    any statue,
And a mouse is miracle enough to stagger sextillions of
    infidels,
And I could come every afternoon of my life to look at

the farmer's girl boiling her iron tea-kettle and baking
shortcake.

I find I incorporate gneiss and coal and long-threaded
    moss and fruits and grains and esculent roots,
And am stucco'd with quadrupeds and birds all over,
And have distanced what is behind me for good reasons,
And call any thing close again when I desire it.

In vain the speeding or shyness,
In vain the plutonic rocks send their old heat against my
    approach,
In vain the mastodon retreats beneath its own powdered
    bones,
In vain objects stand leagues off and assume manifold
    shapes,
In vain the ocean settling in hollows and the great
    monsters lying low,
In vain the buzzard houses herself with the sky,
In vain the snake slides through the creepers and logs,
In vain the elk takes to the inner passes of the woods,
In vain the razorbilled auk sails far north to Labrador,
I follow quickly . . . . I ascend to the nest in the fissure
    of the cliff.

[32]
I think I could turn and live awhile with the animals
    . . . . they are so placid and self-contained,
I stand and look at them sometimes half the day long.

They do not sweat and whine about their condition,
They do not lie awake in the dark and weep for their
    sins,

They do not make me sick discussing their duty to
    God,
Not one is dissatisfied . . . . not one is demented with
    the mania of owning things,
Not one kneels to another nor to his kind that lived
    thousands of years ago,
Not one is respectable or industrious over the whole
    earth.

So they show their relations to me and I accept them;
They bring me tokens of myself . . . . they evince them
    plainly in their possession.

I do not know where they got those tokens,
I must have passed that way untold times ago and
    negligently dropt them,
Myself moving forward then and now and forever,
Gathering and showing more always and with velocity,
Infinite and omnigenous and the like of these among
    them;
Not too exclusive toward the reachers of my
    remembrancers,
Picking out here one that shall be my amie,
Choosing to go with him on brotherly terms.

A gigantic beauty of a stallion, fresh and responsive to my
    caresses,
Head high in the forehead and wide between the ears,
Limbs glossy and supple, tail dusting the ground,
Eyes well apart and full of sparkling wickedness . . . . ears
    finely cut and flexibly moving.

His nostrils dilate . . . . my heels embrace him . . . . his

42

well built limbs tremble with pleasure . . . . we speed
around and return.

I but use you a moment and then I resign you stallion
    . . . . and do not need your paces, and outgallop
    them,
And myself as I stand or sit pass faster than you.

[33]
Swift wind! Space! My Soul! Now I know it is true what
    I guessed at;
What I guessed when I loafed on the grass,
What I guessed while I lay alone in my bed . . . . and
    again as I walked the beach under the paling stars of
    the morning.

My ties and ballasts leave me . . . . I travel . . . . I sail
    . . . . my elbows rest in the sea-gaps,
I skirt the sierras . . . . my palms cover continents,
I am afoot with my vision.

By the city's quadrangular houses . . . . in log-huts, or
    camping with lumbermen,
Along the ruts of the turnpike . . . . along the dry gulch
    and rivulet bed,
Hoeing my onion-patch, and rows of carrots and
    parsnips . . . . crossing savannas . . . . trailing in forests,
Prospecting . . . . gold-digging . . . . girdling the trees of
    a new purchase,
Scorched ankle-deep by the hot sand . . . . hauling my
    boat down the shallow river;
Where the panther walks to and fro on a limb overhead
    . . . . where the buck turns furiously at the hunter,

43

Where the rattlesnake suns his flabby length on a rock
    . . . . where the otter is feeding on fish,
Where the alligator in his tough pimples sleeps by the
    bayou,
Where the black bear is searching for roots or honey
    . . . . where the beaver pats the mud with his paddle-
    tail;
Over the growing sugar . . . . over the cottonplant . . . .
    over the rice in its low moist field;
Over the sharp-peaked farmhouse with its scalloped scum
    and slender shoots from the gutters;
Over the western persimmon . . . . over the longleaved
    corn and the delicate blue-flowered flax;
Over the white and brown buckwheat, a hummer and a
    buzzer there with the rest,
Over the dusky green of the rye as it ripples and shades
    in the breeze;
Scaling mountains . . . . pulling myself cautiously up
    . . . . holding on by low scragged limbs,
Walking the path worn in the grass and beat through the
    leaves of the brush;
Where the quail is whistling betwixt the woods and the
    wheatlot,
Where the bat flies in the July eve . . . . where the great
    goldbug drops through the dark;
Where the flails keep time on the barn floor,
Where the brook puts out of the roots of the old tree
    and flows to the meadow,
Where the cattle stand and shake away flies with the
    tremulous shuddering of their hides,
Where the cheese-cloth hangs in the kitchen, and
    andirons straddle the hearth-slab, and cobwebs fall in
    festoons from the rafters;

Where triphammers crash . . . . where the press is
whirling its cylinders;
Wherever the human heart beats with terrible throes out
of its ribs;
Where the pear-shaped balloon is floating aloft . . . .
floating in it myself and looking composedly down;
Where the life-car is drawn on the slipnoose . . . . where
the heat hatches pale-green eggs in the dented sand,
Where the she-whale swims with her calves and never
forsakes them,
Where the steamship trails hindways its long pennant of
smoke,
Where the ground-shark's fin cuts like a black chip out
of the water,
Where the half-burned brig is riding on unknown
currents,
Where shells grow to her slimy deck, and the dead are
corrupting below;
Where the striped and starred flag is borne at the head of
the regiments;
Approaching Manhattan, up by the long-stretching island,
Under Niagara, the cataract falling like a veil over my
countenance;
Upon a door-step . . . . upon the horse-block of hard
wood outside,
Upon the race-course, or enjoying pic-nics or jigs or a
good game of base-ball,
At he-festivals with blackguard jibes and ironical license
and bull-dances and drinking and laughter,
At the cider-mill, tasting the sweet of the brown sqush
. . . . sucking the juice through a straw,
At apple-peelings, wanting kisses for all the red fruit I
find,

At musters and beach-parties and friendly bees and
huskings and house-raisings;
Where the mockingbird sounds his delicious gurgles, and
cackles and screams and weeps,
Where the hay-rick stands in the barnyard, and the
dry-stalks are scattered, and the brood cow waits in
the hovel,
Where the bull advances to do his masculine work, and
the stud to the mare, and the cock is treading the hen,
Where the heifers browse, and the geese nip their food
with short jerks;
Where the sundown shadows lengthen over the limitless
and lonesome prairie,
Where the herds of buffalo make a crawling spread of the
square miles far and near;
Where the hummingbird shimmers . . . . where the neck
of the longlived swan is curving and winding;
Where the laughing-gull scoots by the slappy shore and
laughs her near-human laugh;
Where beehives range on a gray bench in the garden
half-hid by the high weeds;
Where the band-necked partridges roost in a ring on the
ground with their heads out;
Where burial coaches enter the arched gates of a
cemetery;
Where winter wolves bark amid wastes of snow and
icicled trees;
Where the yellow-crowned heron comes to the edge of
the marsh at night and feeds upon small crabs;
Where the splash of swimmers and divers cools the warm
noon;
Where the katydid works her chromatic reed on the
walnut-tree over the well;

Through patches of citrons and cucumbers with silver-
wired leaves,
Through the salt-lick or orange glade . . . . or under
conical firs;
Through the gymnasium . . . . through the curtained
saloon . . . . through the office or public hall;
Pleased with the native and pleased with the foreign
. . . . pleased with the new and old,
Pleased with women, the homely as well as the
handsome,
Pleased with the quakeress as she puts off her bonnet and
talks melodiously,
Pleased with the primitive tunes of the choir of the
whitewashed church,
Pleased with the earnest words of the sweating Methodist
preacher, or any preacher . . . . looking seriously at
the camp-meeting;
Looking in at the shop-windows in Broadway the whole
forenoon . . . . pressing the flesh of my nose to the
thick plate-glass,
Wandering the same afternoon with my face turned up
to the clouds;
My right and left arms round the sides of two friends
and I in the middle;
Coming home with the bearded and dark-cheeked
bush-boy . . . . riding behind him at the drape of the
day;
Far from the settlements studying the print of animals'
feet, or the moccasin print;
By the cot in the hospital reaching lemonade to a
feverish patient,
By the coffined corpse when all is still, examining with a
candle;

Voyaging to every port to dicker and adventure;

Hurrying with the modern crowd, as eager and fickle as any,

Hot toward one I hate, ready in my madness to knife him;

Solitary at midnight in my back yard, my thoughts gone from me a long while,

Walking the old hills of Judea with the beautiful gentle god by my side;

Speeding through space . . . . speeding through heaven and the stars,

Speeding amid the seven satellites and the broad ring and the diameter of eighty thousand miles,

Speeding with tailed meteors . . . . throwing fire-balls like the rest,

Carrying the crescent child that carries its own full mother in its belly:

Storming enjoying planning loving cautioning,

Backing and filling, appearing and disappearing,

I tread day and night such roads.

I visit the orchards of God and look at the spheric product,

And look at quintillions ripened, and look at quintillions green.

I fly the flight of the fluid and swallowing soul,

My course runs below the soundings of plummets.

I help myself to material and immaterial,

No guard can shut me off, no law can prevent me.

I anchor my ship for a little while only,

My messengers continually cruise away or bring their
    returns to me.

I go hunting polar furs and the seal . . . . leaping chasms
    with a pike-pointed staff . . . . clinging to topples of
    brittle and blue.

I ascend to the foretruck . . . . I take my place late at
    night in the crow's nest . . . . we sail through the
    arctic sea . . . . it is plenty light enough,
Through the clear atmosphere I stretch around on the
    wonderful beauty,
The enormous masses of ice pass me and I pass them
    . . . . the scenery is plain in all directions,
The white-topped mountains point up in the distance
    . . . . I fling out my fancies toward them;
We are about approaching some great battlefield in which
    we are soon to be engaged,
We pass the colossal outposts of the encampment . . . .
    we pass with still feet and caution;
Or we are entering by the suburbs some vast and ruined
    city . . . . the blocks and fallen architecture more
    than all the living cities of the globe.

I am a free companion . . . . I bivouac by invading watchfires.

I turn the bridegroom out of bed and stay with the bride
    myself,
And tighten her all night to my thighs and lips.

My voice is the wife's voice, the screech by the rail of
    the stairs,
They fetch my man's body up dripping and drowned.

I understand the large hearts of heroes,
The courage of present times and all times;
How the skipper saw the crowded and rudderless wreck
    of the steamship, and death chasing it up and down
    the storm,
How he knuckled tight and gave not back one inch, and
    was faithful of days and faithful of nights,
And chalked in large letters on a board, Be of good
    cheer, We will not desert you;
How he saved the drifting company at last,
How the lank loose-gowned women looked when boated
    from the side of their prepared graves,
How the silent old-faced infants, and the lifted sick, and
    the sharplipped unshaved men;
All this I swallow and it tastes good . . . . I like it well,
    and it becomes mine,
I am the man . . . . I suffered . . . . I was there.


The disdain and calmness of martyrs,
The mother condemned for a witch and burnt with dry
    wood, and her children gazing on;
The hounded slave that flags in the race and leans by the
    fence, blowing and covered with sweat,
The twinges that string like needles his legs and neck,
The murderous buckshot and the bullets,
All these I feel or am.


I am the hounded slave . . . . I wince at the bite of the
    dogs,
Hell and despair are upon me . . . . crack and again
    crack the marksmen,
I clutch the rails of the fence . . . . my gore dribs
    thinned with the ooze of my skin,

I fall on the weeds and stones,
The riders spur their unwilling horses and haul close,
They taunt my dizzy ears . . . . they beat me violently
    over the head with their whip-stocks.

Agonies are one of my changes of garments;
I do not ask the wounded person how he feels . . . . I
    myself become the wounded person,
My hurt turns livid upon me as I lean on a cane and
    observe.

I am the mashed fireman with breastbone broken . . . .
    tumbling walls buried me in their debris,
Heat and smoke I inspired . . . . I heard the yelling
    shouts of my comrades,
I heard the distant click of their picks and shovels;
They have cleared the beams away . . . . they tenderly lift
    me forth.

I lie in the night air in my red shirt . . . . the pervading
    hush is for my sake,
Painless after all I lie, exhausted but not so unhappy,
White and beautiful are the faces around me . . . . the
    heads are bared of their fire-caps,
The kneeling crowd fades with the light of the torches.

Distant and dead resuscitate,
They show as the dial or move as the hands of me . . . .
    and I am the clock myself.

I am an old artillerist, and tell of some fort's
    bombardment . . . . and am there again.

Again the reveille of drummers . . . . again the attacking
    cannon and mortars and howitzers,
Again the attacked send their cannon responsive.

I take part . . . . I see and hear the whole,
The cries and curses and roar . . . . the plaudits for well
    aimed shots,
The ambulanza slowly passing and training its red drip,
Workmen searching after damages and to make
    indispensable repairs,
The fall of grenades through the rent roof . . . . the
    fan-shaped explosion,
The whizz of limbs heads stone wood and iron high in
    the air.

Again gurgles the mouth of my dying general . . . . he
    furiously waves with his hand,
He gasps through the clot . . . . Mind not me . . . .
    mind . . . . the entrenchments.

[34]
I tell not the fall of Alamo . . . . not one escaped to tell
    the fall of Alamo,
The hundred and fifty are dumb yet at Alamo.

Hear now the tale of a jetblack sunrise,
Hear of the murder in cold blood of four hundred and
    twelve young men.

Retreating they had formed in a hollow square with their
    baggage for breastworks,
Nine hundred lives out of the surrounding enemy's nine
    times their number was the price they took in advance,

Their colonel was wounded and their ammunition gone,
They treated for an honorable capitulation, received
    writing and seal, gave up their arms, and marched
    back prisoners of war.

They were the glory of the race of rangers,
Matchless with a horse, a rifle, a song, a supper or a
    courtship,
Large, turbulent, brave, handsome, generous, proud and
    affectionate,
Bearded, sunburnt, dressed in the free costume of hunters,
Not a single one over thirty years of age.

The second Sunday morning they were brought out in
    squads and massacred . . . . it was beautiful early
    summer,
The work commenced about five o'clock and was over
    by eight.

None obeyed the command to kneel,
Some made a mad and helpless rush . . . . some stood
    stark and straight,
A few fell at once, shot in the temple or heart . . . . the
    living and dead lay together,
The maimed and mangled dug in the dirt . . . . the
    new-comers saw them there;
Some half-killed attempted to crawl away,
These were dispatched with bayonets or battered with the
    blunts of muskets;
A youth not seventeen years old seized his assassin till
    two more came to release him,
The three were all torn, and covered with the boys
    blood.

At eleven o'clock began the burning of the bodies;
And that is the tale of the murder of the four hundred
    and twelve young men,
And that was a jetblack sunrise.


[35]
Did you read in the seabooks of the oldfashioned frigate-
    fight?
Did you learn who won by the light of the moon and
    stars?


Our foe was no skulk in his ship, I tell you,
His was the English pluck, and there is no tougher or
    truer, and never was, and never will be;
Along the lowered eve he came, horribly raking us.


We closed with him . . . . the yards entangled . . . . the
    cannon touched,
My captain lashed fast with his own hands.


We had received some eighteen-pound shots under the
    water,
On our lower-gun-deck two large pieces had burst at
    the first fire, killing all around and blowing up
    overhead.


Ten o'clock at night, and the full moon shining and the
    leaks on the gain, and five feet of water reported,
The master-at-arms loosing the prisoners confined in the
    after-hold to give them a chance for themselves.


The transit to and from the magazine was now stopped
    by the sentinels,

They saw so many strange faces they did not know
    whom to trust.

Our frigate was afire . . . . the other asked if we
    demanded quarter? if our colors were struck and the
    fighting done?

I laughed content when I heard the voice of my little
    captain,
We have not struck, he composedly cried, We have just
    begun our part of the fighting.

Only three guns were in use,
One was directed by the captain himself against the
    enemy's mainmast,
Two well-served with grape and canister silenced his
    musketry and cleared his decks.

The tops alone seconded the fire of this little battery,
    especially the maintop,
They all held out bravely during the whole of the
    action.

Not a moment's cease,
The leaks gained fast on the pumps . . . . the fire eats
    toward the powder-magazine,
One of the pumps was shot away . . . . it was generally
    thought we were sinking.

Serene stood the little captain,
He was not hurried . . . . his voice was neither high nor
    low,
His eyes gave more light to us than our battle-lanterns.

Toward twelve at night, there in the beams of the moon
    they surrendered to us.

[36]
Stretched and still lay the midnight,
Two great hulls motionless on the breast of the darkness,
Our vessel riddled and slowly sinking . . . . preparations
    to pass to the one we had conquered,
The captain on the quarter deck coldly giving his orders
    through a countenance white as a sheet,
Near by the corpse of the child that served in the
    cabin,
The dead face of an old salt with long white hair and
    carefully curled whiskers,
The flames spite of all that could be done flickering aloft
    and below,
The husky voices of the two or three officers yet fit for
    duty,
Formless stacks of bodies and bodies by themselves . . . .
    dabs of flesh upon the masts and spars,
The cut of cordage and dangle of rigging . . . . the slight
    shock of the soothe of waves,
Black and impressive guns, and litter of powder-parcels,
    and the strong scent,
Delicate sniffs of the seabreeze . . . . smells of sedgy grass
    and fields by the shore . . . . death-messages given in
    charge to survivors,
The hiss of the surgeon's knife and the gnawing teeth of
    his saw,
The wheeze, the cluck, the swash of falling blood . . . .
    the short wild scream, the long dull tapering groan,
These so . . . . these irretrievable.

O Christ! My fit is mastering me!
What the rebel said gaily adjusting his throat to the rope-
     noose,
What the savage at the stump, his eye-sockets empty, his
     mouth spirting whoops and defiance,
What stills the traveler come to the vault at Mount
     Vernon,
What sobers the Brooklyn boy as he looks down the
     shores of the Wallabout and remembers the prison
     ships,
What burnt the gums of the redcoat at Saratoga when he
     surrendered his brigades,
These become mine and me every one, and they are but
     little,
I become as much more as I like.

I become any presence or truth of humanity here,
And see myself in prison shaped like another man,
And feel the dull unintermitted pain.

For me the keepers of convicts shoulder their carbines
     and keep watch,
It is I let out in the morning and barred at night.

Not a mutineer walks handcuffed to jail, but I am
     handcuffed to him and walk by his side,
I am less the jolly one there, and more the silent one
     with sweat on my twitching lips.

Not a youngster is taken for larceny, but I go too and am
     tried and sentenced.

Not a cholera patient lies at the last gasp, but I also lie at
the last gasp,
My face is ash-colored, my sinews gnarl . . . . away from
me people retreat.

Askers embody themselves in me, and I am embodied in
them,
I project my hat and sit shamefaced and beg.

I rise extatic through all, and sweep with the true
gravitation,
The whirling and whirling is elemental within me.

[38]
Somehow I have been stunned. Stand back!
Give me a little time beyond my cuffed head and
slumbers and dreams and gaping,
I discover myself on a verge of the usual mistake.

That I could forget the mockers and insults!
That I could forget the trickling tears and the blows of
the bludgeons and hammers!
That I could look with a separate look on my own
crucifixion and bloody crowning!

I remember . . . . I resume the overstaid fraction,
The grave of rock multiplies what has been confided to
it . . . . or to any graves,
The corpses rise . . . . the gashes heal . . . . the
fastenings roll away.

I troop forth replenished with supreme power, one of an
average unending procession,

We walk the roads of Ohio and Massachusetts and
    Virginia and Wisconsin and New York and New
    Orleans and Texas and Montreal and San Francisco
    and Charleston and Savannah and Mexico,
Inland and by the seacoast and boundary lines . . . . and
    we pass the boundary lines.

Our swift ordinances are on their way over the whole earth,
The blossoms we wear in our hats are the growth of two
    thousand years.

Eleves I salute you,
I see the approach of your numberless gangs . . . . I see
    you understand yourselves and me,
And know that they who have eyes are divine, and the
    blind and lame are equally divine,
And that my steps drag behind yours yet go before them,
And are aware how I am with you no more than I am
    with everybody.

[39]
The friendly and flowing savage . . . . Who is he?
Is he waiting for civilization or past it and mastering it?

Is he some southwesterner raised outdoors? Is he
    Canadian?
Is he from the Mississippi country? or from Iowa, Oregon
    or California? or from the mountain? or prairie life
    or bush-life? or from the sea?

Wherever he goes men and women accept and desire him,
They desire he should like them and touch them and
    speak to them and stay with them.

Behaviour lawless as snow-flakes . . . . words simple as
    grass . . . . uncombed head and laughter and naiveté;
Slowstepping feet and the common features, and the
    common modes and emanations,
They descend in new forms from the tips of his fingers,
They are wafted with the odor of his body or breath
    . . . . they fly out of the glance of his eyes.

[40]
Flaunt of the sunshine I need not your bask . . . . lie
    over,
You light surfaces only . . . . I force the surfaces and the
    depths also.

Earth! you seem to look for something at my hands,
Say old topknot! what do you want?

Man or woman! I might tell how I like you, but cannot,
And might tell what it is in me and what it is in you,
    but cannot,
And might tell the pinings I have . . . . the pulse of my
    nights and days.

Behold I do not give lectures or a little charity,
What I give I give out of myself.

You there, impotent, loose in the knees, open your
    scarfed chops till I blow grit within you,
Spread your palms and lift the flaps of your pockets,
I am not to be denied . . . . I compel . . . . I have stores
    plenty and to spare,
And any thing I have I bestow.

I do not ask who you are . . . . that is not important to
  me,
You can do nothing and be nothing but what I will
  infold you.

To a drudge of the cottonfields or emptier of privies I
  lean . . . . on his right cheek I put the family kiss,
And in my soul I swear I never will deny him.

On women fit for conception I start bigger and nimbler
  babes,
This day I am jetting the stuff of far more arrogant
  republics.

To any one dying . . . . thither I speed and twist the
  knob of the door,
Turn the bedclothes toward the foot of the bed,
Let the physician and the priest go home.

I seize the descending man . . . . I raise him with
  resistless will.

O despairer, here is my neck,
By God! you shall not go down! Hang your whole
  weight upon me.

I dilate you with tremendous breath . . . . I buoy you up;
Every room of the house do I fill with an armed force
  . . . . lovers of me, bafflers of graves:
Sleep! I and they keep guard all night;
Not doubt, not decease shall dare to lay finger upon you,
I have embraced you, and henceforth possess you to
  myself,

And when you rise in the morning you will find what I
    tell you is so.

[41]
I am he bringing help for the sick as they pant on their
    backs,
And for strong upright men I bring yet more needed
    help.

I heard what was said of the universe,
Heard it and heard of several thousand years;
It is middling well as far as it goes . . . . but is that all?

Magnifying and applying come I,
Outbidding at the start the old cautious hucksters,
The most they offer for mankind and eternity less than a
    spirit of my own seminal wet,
Taking myself the exact dimensions of Jehovah and laying
    them away,
Lithographing Kronos and Zeus his son, and Hercules his
    grandson,
Buying drafts of Osiris and Isis and Belus and Brahma
    and Adonai,
In my portfolio placing Manito loose, and Allah on a leaf,
    and the crucifix engraved,
With Odin, and the hideous-faced Mexitli, and all idols
    and images,
Honestly taking them all for what they are worth, and
    not a cent more,
Admitting they were alive and did the work of their day,
Admitting they bore mites as for unfledged birds who
    have now to rise and fly and sing for themselves,
Accepting the rough deific sketches to fill out better in

myself . . . . bestowing them freely on each man and woman I see,

Discovering as much or more in a framer framing a house,

Putting higher claims for him there with his rolled-up sleeves, driving the mallet and chisel;

Not objecting to special revelations . . . . considering a curl of smoke or a hair on the back of my hand as curious as any revelation;

Those ahold of fire-engines and hook-and-ladder ropes more to me than the gods of the antique wars,

Minding their voices peal through the crash of destruction,

Their brawny limbs passing safe over charred laths . . . . their white foreheads whole and unhurt out of the flames;

By the mechanic's wife with her babe at her nipple interceding for every person born;

Three scythes at harvest whizzing in a row from three lusty angels with shirts bagged out at their waists;

The snag-toothed hostler with red hair redeeming sins past and to come,

Selling all he possesses and traveling on foot to fee lawyers for his brother and sit by him while he is tried for forgery:

What was strewn in the amplest strewing the square rod about me, and not filling the square rod then;

The bull and the bug never worshipped half enough,

Dung and dirt more admirable than was dreamed,

The supernatural of no account . . . . myself waiting my time to be one of the supremes,

The day getting ready for me when I shall do as much good as the best, and be as prodigious,

Guessing when I am it will not tickle me much to
    receive puffs out of pulpit or print;
By my life-lumps! becoming already a creator!
Putting myself here and now to the ambushed womb of
    the shadows!

[42]
. . . . A call in the midst of the crowd,
My own voice, orotund sweeping and final.

Come my children,
Come my boys and girls, and my women and household
    and intimates,
Now the performer launches his nerve . . . . he has
    passed his prelude on the reeds within.

Easily written loosefingered chords! I feel the thrum of
    their climax and close.

My head evolves on my neck,
Music rolls, but not from the organ . . . . folks are around
    me, but they are no household of mine.

Ever the hard and unsunk ground,
Ever the eaters and drinkers . . . . ever the upward and
    downward sun . . . . ever the air and the ceaseless
    tides,
Ever myself and my neighbors, refreshing and wicked and
    real,
Ever the old inexplicable query . . . . ever that thorned
    thumb—that breath of itches and thirsts,
Ever the vexers hoot! hoot! till we find where the sly
    one hides and bring him forth;

Ever love . . . . ever the sobbing liquid of life,
Ever the bandage under the chin . . . . ever the trestles of
    death.

Here and there with dimes on the eyes walking,
To feed the greed of the belly the brains liberally
    spooning,
Tickets buying or taking or selling, but in to the feast
    never once going;
Many sweating and ploughing and thrashing, and then
    the chaff for payment receiving,
A few idly owning, and they the wheat continually
    claiming.

This is the city . . . . and I am one of the citizens;
Whatever interests the rest interests me . . . . politics,
    churches, newspapers, schools,
Benevolent societies, improvements, banks, tariffs,
    steamships, factories, markets,
Stocks and stores and real estate and personal estate.

They who piddle and patter here in collars and tailed
    coats . . . . I am aware who they are . . . . and that
    they are not worms or fleas,
I acknowledge the duplicates of myself under all the
    scrape-lipped and pipe-legged concealments.

The weakest and shallowest is deathless with me,
What I do and say the same waits for them,
Every thought that flounders in me the same flounders in
    them.

I know perfectly well my own egotism,

And know my omnivorous words, and cannot say any less.
And would fetch you whoever you are flush with myself.

My words are words of a questioning, and to indicate
reality;
This printed and bound book . . . . but the printer and
the printing-office boy?
The marriage estate and settlement . . . . but the body
and mind of the bridegroom? also those of the bride?
The panorama of the sea . . . . but the sea itself?
The well-taken photographs . . . . but your wife or friend
close and solid in your arms?
The fleet of ships of the line and all the modern
improvements . . . . but the craft and pluck of the
admiral?
The dishes and fare and furniture . . . . but the host and
hostess, and the look out of their eyes?
The sky up there . . . . yet here or next door or across
the way?
The saints and sages in history . . . . but you yourself?
Sermons and creeds and theology . . . . but the human
brain, and what is called reason, and what is called
love, and what is called life?

[43]
I do not despise you priests;
My faith is the greatest of faiths and the least of faiths,
Enclosing all worship ancient and modern, and all
between ancient and modern,
Believing I shall come again upon the earth after five
thousand years,
Waiting responses from oracles . . . . honoring the gods
. . . . saluting the sun,

Making a fetish of the first rock or stump . . . . powowing
   with sticks in the circle of obis,
Helping the lama or brahmin as he trims the lamps of
   the idols,
Dancing yet through the streets in a phallic procession
   . . . . rapt and austere in the woods, a gymnosophist,
Drinking mead from the skull-cup . . . . to shasta and
   vedas admirant . . . . minding the koran,
Walking the toekallis, spotted with gore from the stone
   and knife . . . . beating the serpent-skin drum;
Accepting the gospels, accepting him that was crucified,
   knowing assuredly that he is divine,
To the mass kneeling . . . . to the puritan's prayer
   rising . . . . sitting patiently in a pew,
Ranting and frothing in my insane crisis . . . . waiting
   dead-like till my spirit arouses me;
Looking forth on pavement and land, and outside of
   pavement and land,
Belonging to the winders of the circuit of circuits.

One of that centripetal and centrifugal gang,
I turn and talk like a man leaving charges before a journey.

Down-hearted doubters, dull and excluded,
Frivolous sullen moping angry affected disheartened
   atheistical,
I know every one of you, and know the unspoken
   interrogatories,
By experience I know them.

How the flukes splash!
How they contort rapid as lightning, with spasms and
   spouts of blood!

Be at peace bloody flukes of doubters and sullen mopers,
I take my place among you as much as among any;
The past is the push of you and me and all precisely the
    same,
And the day and night are for you and me and all,
And what is yet untried and afterward is for you and me
    and all.

I do not know what is untried and afterward,
But I know it is sure and alive and sufficient.

Each who passes is considered, and each who stops is
    considered, and not a single one can it fail.

It cannot fail the young man who died and was buried,
Nor the young woman who died and was put by his
    side,
Nor the little child that peeped in at the door and then
    drew back and was never seen again,
Nor the old man who has lived without purpose, and
    feels it with bitterness worse than gall,
Nor him in the poorhouse tubercled by rum and the bad
    disorder,
Nor the numberless slaughtered and wrecked . . . . nor
    the brutish koboo, called the ordure of humanity,
Nor the sacs merely floating with open mouths for food
    to slip in,
Nor any thing in the earth, or down in the oldest graves
    of the earth,
Nor any thing in the myriads of spheres, nor one of the
    myriads of myriads that inhabit them,
Nor the present, nor the least wisp that is known.

[44]
It is time to explain myself . . . . let us stand up.

What is known I strip away . . . . I launch all men and
    women forward with me into the unknown.

The clock indicates the moment . . . . but what does
    eternity indicate?

Eternity lies in bottomless reservoirs . . . . its buckets are
    rising forever and ever,
They pour and they pour and they exhale away.

We have thus far exhausted trillions of winters and
    summers;
There are trillions ahead, and trillions ahead of them.

Births have brought us richness and variety,
And other births will bring us richness and variety.

I do not call one greater and one smaller,
That which fills its period and place is equal to any.

Were mankind murderous or jealous upon you my
    brother or my sister?
I am sorry for you . . . . they are not murderous or
    jealous upon me;
All has been gentle with me . . . . I keep no account
    with lamentation; What have I to do with
    lamentation?

I am an acme of things accomplished, and I an encloser
    of things to be.

My feet strike an apex of the apices of the stairs,
On every step bunches of ages, and larger bunches
    between the steps,
All below duly traveled . . . . and still I mount and
    mount.

Rise after rise bow the phantoms behind me,
Afar down I see the huge first Nothing, the vapor from
    the nostrils of death,
I know I was even there . . . . I waited unseen and always,
And slept while God carried me through the lethargic mist,
And took my time . . . . and took no hurt from the
    foetid carbon.

Long I was hugged close . . . . long and long.

Immense have been the preparations for me,
Faithful and friendly the arms that have helped me.

Cycles ferried my cradle, rowing and rowing like cheerful
    boatmen;
For room to me stars kept aside in their own rings,
They sent influences to look after what was to hold me.

Before I was born out of my mother generations guided
    me,
My embryo has never been torpid . . . . nothing could
    overlay it;
For it the nebula cohered to an orb . . . . the long slow
    strata piled to rest it on . . . . vast vegetables gave it
    sustenance,
Monstrous sauroids transported it in their mouths and
    deposited it with care.

All forces have been steadily employed to complete and
    delight me,
Now I stand on this spot with my soul.

[45]
Span of youth! Ever-pushed elasticity! Manhood balanced
    and florid and full!

My lovers suffocate me!
Crowding my lips, and thick in the pores of my skin,
Jostling me through streets and public halls .... coming
    naked to me at night,
Crying by day Ahoy from the rocks of the river ....
    swinging and chirping over my head,
Calling my name from flowerbeds or vines or tangled
    underbrush,
Or while I swim in the bath.... or drink from the
    pump at the corner.... or the curtain is down at the
    opera.... or I glimpse at a womans face in the
    railroad car;
Lighting on every moment of my life,
Bussing my body with soft and balsamic busses,
Noiselessly passing handfuls out of their hearts and giving
    them to be mine.

Old age superbly rising! Ineffable grace of dying days!

Every condition promulges not only itself.... it
    promulges what grows after and out of itself,
And the dark hush promulges as much as any.

I open my scuttle at night and see the far-sprinkled
    systems,

And all I see, multiplied as high as I can cipher, edge but
    the rim of the farther systems.

Wider and wider they spread, expanding and always
    expanding,
Outward and outward and forever outward.

My sun has his sun, and round him obediently wheels,
He joins with his partners a group of superior circuit,
And greater sets follow, making specks of the greatest
    inside them.

There is no stoppage, and never can be stoppage;
If I and you and the worlds and all beneath or upon
    their surfaces, and all the palpable life, were this
    moment reduced back to a pallid float, it would not
    avail in the long run,
We should surely bring up again where we now stand,
And as surely go as much farther, and then farther and
    farther.

A few quadrillions of eras, a few octillions of cubic
    leagues, do not hazard the span, or make it impatient,
They are but parts . . . . any thing is but a part.

See ever so far . . . . there is limitless space outside of
    that,
Count ever so much . . . . there is limitless time around
    that.

Our rendezvous is fitly appointed . . . . God will be there
    and wait till we come.

I know I have the best of time and space—and that I was
    never measured, and never will be measured.

I tramp a perpetual journey,
My signs are a rain-proof coat and good shoes and a staff
    cut from the woods;
No friend of mine takes his ease in my chair,
I have no chair, nor church nor philosophy;
I lead no man to a dinner-table or library or exchange,
But each man and each woman of you I lead upon a
    knoll,
My left hand hooks you round the waist,
My right hand points to landscapes of continents, and a
    plain public road.

Not I, not any one else can travel that road for you,
You must travel it for yourself.

It is not far. . . . it is within reach,
Perhaps you have been on it since you were born, and
    did not know,
Perhaps it is every where on water and on land.

Shoulder your duds, and I will mine, and let us hasten
    forth;
Wonderful cities and free nations we shall fetch as we go.

If you tire, give me both burdens, and rest the chuff of
    your hand on my hip,
And in due time you shall repay the same service to me;
For after we start we never lie by again.

This day before dawn I ascended a hill and looked at the
crowded heaven,
And I said to my spirit, When we become the enfolders
of the those orbs and the pleasure and knowledge of
every thing in them, shall we be filled and satisfied
then?
And my spirit said No, we level that lift to pass and
continue beyond.

You are also asking me questions, and I hear you;
I answer that I cannot answer . . . . you must find out for
yourself.

Sit awhile wayfarer,
Here are biscuits to eat and here is milk to drink,
But as soon as you sleep and renew yourself in sweet
clothes I will certainly kiss you with my goodbye kiss
and open the gate for your egress hence.

Long enough have you dreamed contemptible dreams,
Now I wash the gum from your eyes,
You must habit yourself to the dazzle of the light and of
every moment of your life.

Long have you timidly waded, holding a plank by the
shore,
Now I will you to be a bold swimmer,
To jump off in the midst of the sea, and rise again and
nod to me and shout, and laughingly dash with your
hair.

[47]
I am the teacher of athletes,
He that by me spreads a wider breast than my own
    proves the width of my own,
He most honors my style who learns under it to destroy
    the teacher.


The boy I love, the same becomes a man not through
    derived power but in his own right,
Wicked, rather than virtuous out of conformity or fear,
Fond of his sweetheart, relishing well his steak,
Unrequited love or a slight cutting him worse than a
    wound cuts,
First rate to ride, to fight, to hit the bull's eye, to sail a
    skiff, to sing a song or play on the banjo,
Preferring scars and faces pitted with smallpox over all
    latherers and those that keep out of the sun.


I teach straying from me, yet who can stray from me?
I follow you whoever you are from the present hour;
My words itch at your ears till you understand them.


I do not say these things for a dollar, or to fill up the
    time while I wait for a boat;
It is you talking just as much as myself . . . . I act as the
    tongue of you,
It was tied in your mouth . . . . in mine it begins to be
    loosened.


I swear I will never mention love or death inside a house,
And I swear I never will translate myself at all, only to
    him or her who privately stays with me in the open
    air.

75

If you would understand me go to the heights or water-
  shore,
The nearest gnat is an explanation and a drop or the
  motion of waves a key,
The maul the oar and the handsaw second my words.

No shuttered room or school can commune with me,
But roughs and little children better than they.

The young mechanic is closest to me . . . . he knows me
  pretty well,
The woodman that takes his axe and jug with him shall
  take me with him all day,
The farmboy ploughing in the field feels good at the
  sound of my voice,
In vessels that sail my words must sail . . . . I go with
  fishermen and seamen, and love them,
My face rubs to the hunter's face when he lies down
  alone in his blanket,
The driver thinking of me does not mind the jolt of his
  wagon,
The young mother and old mother shall comprehend
  me,
The girl and the wife rest the needle a moment and
  forget where they are,
They and all would resume what I have told them.

[48]
I have said that the soul is not more than the body,
And I have said that the body is not more than the soul,
And nothing, not God, is greater to one than one's-self is,
And whoever walks a furlong without sympathy walks to
  his own funeral, dressed in his shroud,

And I or you pocketless of a dime may purchase the pick
of the earth,
And to glance with an eye or show a bean in its pod
confounds the learning of all times,
And there is no trade or employment but the young man
following it may become a hero,
And there is no object so soft but it makes a hub for the
wheeled universe,
And any man or woman shall stand cool and supercilious
before a million universes.

And I call to mankind, Be not curious about God,
For I who am curious about each am not curious about
God,
No array of terms can say how much I am at peace
about God and about death.

I hear and behold God in every object, yet I understand
God not in the least,
Nor do I understand who there can be more wonderful
than myself.

Why should I wish to see God better than this day?
I see something of God each hour of the twenty-four,
and each moment then,
In the faces of men and women I see God, and in my
own face in the glass;
I find letters from God dropped in the street, and every
one is signed by God's name,
And I leave them where they are, for I know that others
will punctually come forever and ever.

And as to you death, and you bitter hug of mortality . . . .
    it is idle to try to alarm me.

To his work without flinching the accoucheur comes,
I see the elderhand pressing receiving supporting,
I recline by the sills of the exquisite flexible doors . . . .
    and mark the outlet, and mark the relief and escape.

And as to you corpse I think you are good manure, but
    that does not offend me,
I smell the white roses sweetscented and growing,
I reach to the leafy lips. . . . I reach to the polished
    breasts of melons,

And as to you life, I reckon you are the leavings of many
    deaths,
No doubt I have died myself ten thousand times before.

I hear you whispering there O stars of heaven,
O suns . . . . O grass of graves . . . . O perpetual transfers
    and promotions . . . . if you do not say anything how
    can I say anything?

Of the turbid pool that lies in the autumn forest,
Of the moon that descends the steeps of the soughing
    twilight,
Toss, sparkles of day and dusk . . . . toss on the black
    stems that decay in the muck,
Toss to the moaning gibberish of the dry limbs.

I ascend from the moon . . . . I ascend from the night,
And perceive of the ghastly glitter the sunbeams reflected,

And debouch to the steady and central from the offspring
   great or small.

[50]
There is that in me . . . . I do not know what it is . . . .
   but I know it is in me.

Wrenched and sweaty . . . . calm and cool then my body
   becomes;
I sleep . . . . I sleep long.

I do not know it . . . . it is without name . . . . it is a
   word unsaid,
It is not in any dictionary or utterance or symbol.

Something it swings on more than the earth I swing on,
To it the creation is the friend whose embracing awakes
   me.

Perhaps I might tell more . . . . Outlines! I plead for my
   brothers and sisters.

Do you see O my brothers and sisters?
It is not chaos or death . . . . it is form and union and
   plan . . . . it is eternal life . . . . it is happiness.

[51]
The past and present wilt . . . . I have filled them and
   emptied them,
And proceed to fill my next fold of the future.

Listener up there! Here you . . . . what have you to
   confide to me?

Look in my face while I snuff the sidle of evening,
Talk honestly, for no one else hears you, and I stay only a
minute longer.

Do I contradict myself?
Very well then . . . . I contradict myself;
I am large . . . . I contain multitudes.

I concentrate toward them that are nigh . . . . I wait on
the door-slab.

Who has done his day's work and will soonest be
through with his supper?
Who wishes to walk with me?

Will you speak before I am gone? Will you prove already
too late?

[52]
The spotted hawk swoops by and accuses me . . . . he
complains of my gab and my loitering.

I too am not a bit tamed . . . . I too am untranslatable,
I sound my barbaric yawp over the roofs of the world,

The last scud of day holds back for me,
It flings my likeness after the rest and true as any on the
shadowed wilds.
It coaxes me to the vapor and the dusk.

I depart as air . . . . I shake my white locks at the
runaway sun,
I effuse my flesh in eddies and drift it in lacy jags.

I bequeath myself to the dirt to grow from the grass I
    love,
If you want me again look for me under your bootsoles.

You will hardly know who I am or what I mean.
But I shall be good health to you nevertheless,
And filter and fibre your blood.

Failing to fetch me at first keep encouraged,
Missing me one place search another,
I stop some where waiting for you.